JOHN LESLEY

CONTINENTS OF THE WORLD

Antarctica

I0892737

REDBACK publishing

Icebergs p.19

Redback Publishing
Suite 6, 13a Narabang Way,
Belrose NSW 2085
Australia

www.redbackpublishing.com
orders@redbackpublishing.com

ISBN 978-1-761400-95-7

Author: John Lesley
Editor: Caroline Thomas
Designer: Redback Publishing

Original illustrations © Redback Publishing 2025

Originated by Redback Publishing

NATIONAL LIBRARY OF AUSTRALIA

A catalogue record for this book is available from the National Library of Australia

Acknowledgements
Abbreviations: l—left, r—right, b—bottom, t—top, c—centre, m—middle
We would like to thank the following for permission to reproduce photographs (images © Shutterstock unless otherwise stated): p8-9, p32br Aurora, Schnuffel2002, CC BY-SA 4.0 (https://creativecommons.org/licenses/by-sa/4.0), via Wikimedia Commons, p9bl Robert Scott, Herbert Ponting (1870-1935), Public domain, via Wikimedia Commons, p9mr Roald Amundsen, Preus Museum Anders Beer Wilse, CC BY 2.0 (https://creativecommons.org/licenses/by/2.0), via Wikimedia Commons, p14bl South Pole comms office, UnturnedFighter, CC BY-SA 4.0 (https://creativecommons.org/licenses/by-sa/4.0CC BY-SA 4.0 Creative Commons Attribution-Share Alike 4.0), via Wikimedia Commons, p15 icebreaker, Eleanor Scriven, p25mr, p32tr kayaking, Eleanor Scriven, p25br Wiencke Island, Antarctica, Eleanor Scriven, p28t Transantarctic mountains, Hannes Grobe, Alfred Wegener Institute, CC BY-SA 2.5 (https://creativecommons.org/licenses/by-sa/2.5), via Wikimedia Commons p28tl map, https://commons.wikimedia.org/wiki/File:Transantarctic_mountains_highlighted.jpg", NASA, Public domain, via Wikimedia Commons, p28bl Aerial view of the Mount Sidley caldera from the southwest, https://commons.wikimedia.org/wiki/File:MountSidleyCaldera.jpg, via Wikimedia Commons, p29tl Thiel Mountains, Icetent at the English Wikipedia, CC BY-SA 3.0 (http://creativecommons.org/licenses/by-sa/3.0/), via Wikimedia Commons, p29tr Dugdale and Murray Glacier, Commander Jim Waldron USNR (Retired), National Science Foundation, Public domain, via Wikimedia Commons, p29 Antarctica relief ocation map, Alexrk2, CC BY-SA 3.0 (https://creativecommons.org/licenses/by-sa/3.0), via Wikimedia Commons

Contents

Antarctic Wildlife p.26

Commercial Fishing p.30

Earth's 7 Continents

How many continents are there?

There are seven continents

Or are there 5?

Some people group Europe and Asia into one continent called Eurasia, and they combine North and South America into the Americas. According to this method of counting, there are five continents instead of seven.

What is a continent?

A continent is a very large landmass which is separated from others on Earth. Some are separated by oceans, but others have land borders with each other.

Origin of Antarctica

How did the continent of Antarctica form?

The rocky surface of our planet is constantly moving in a process called plate tectonics. As massive blocks of rock separate, they move across the surface of Earth, forming the continents we know today.

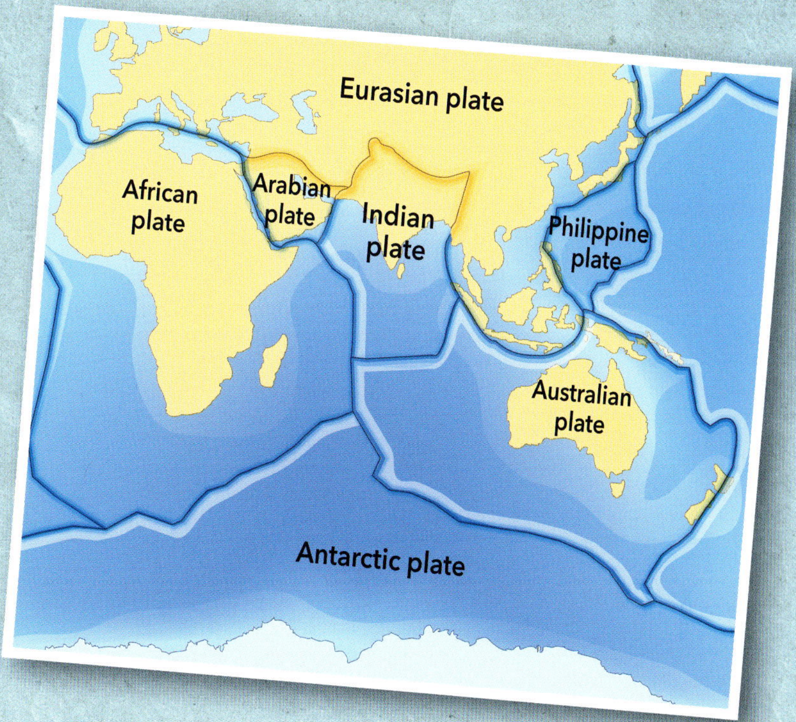

A continent transformed

The continents were not always in the same location as they are now. Millions of years ago, they were parts of different moving pieces of land, two of which were Pangaea and Gondwana. Dinosaur and plant fossils from Antarctica show that there was a time when the continent was ice-free and supported a wide variety of living things.

Millions of years ago, Antarctica had borders with what are now Africa, India and Australia.

The Continent of Antarctica

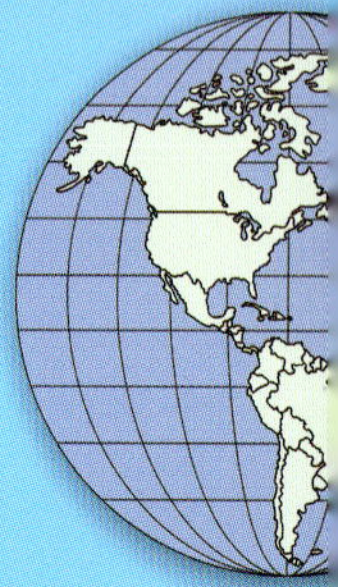

What's underneath the ice?

Underneath Antarctica's covering of ice there is a whole rocky continent. In contrast, the Arctic in the northern polar region is formed from ice floating on top of the sea.

The Antarctic ice sheet is the largest single piece of ice on Earth. It covers millions of square kilometres and contains over 60% of the world's fresh water. The total ice sheet is made up of three very large ice sheets, as well as a number of smaller ones. Glaciers drain the ice and snow from these ice sheets.

Can you believe this?

At its deepest, the Antarctic ice sheet is nearly five kilometres thick!

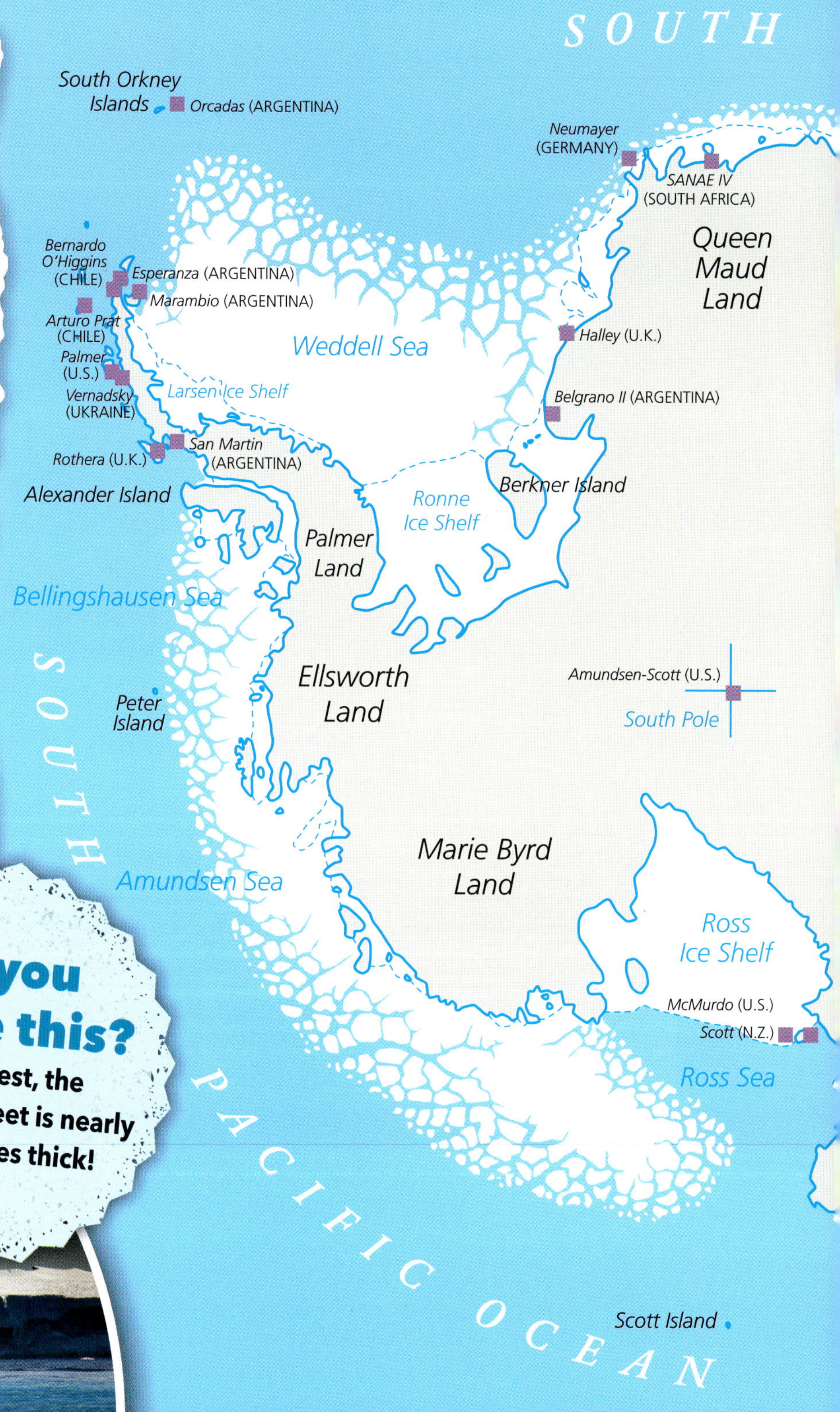

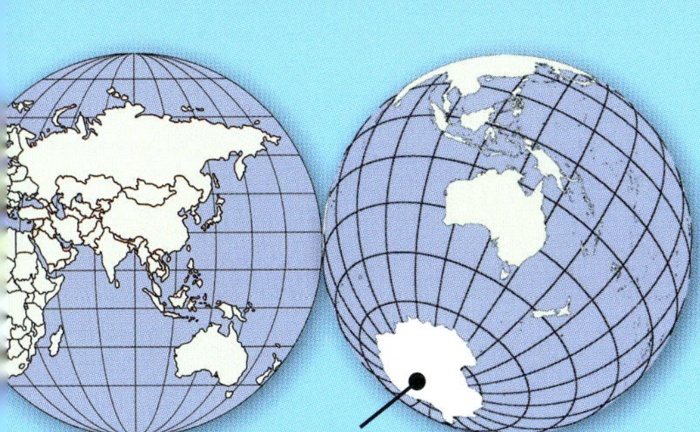

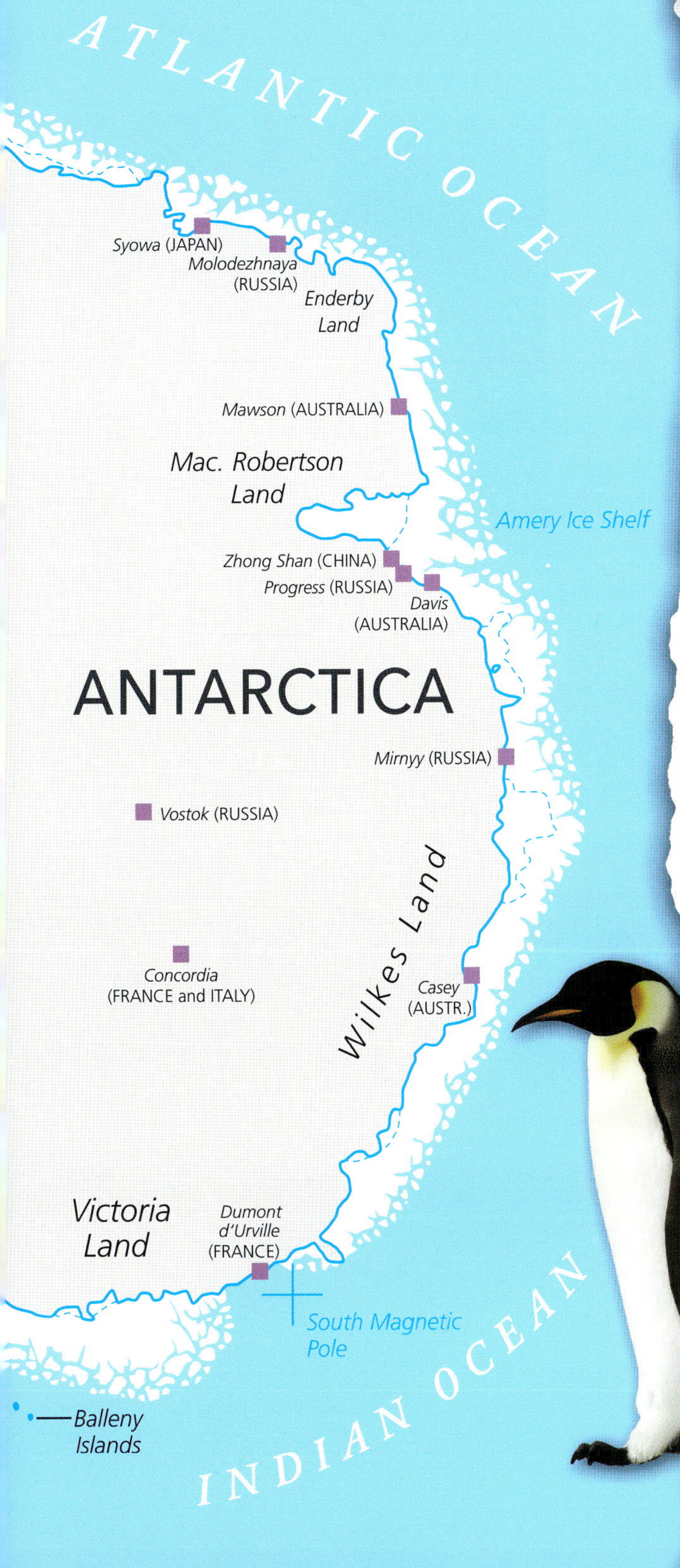

How Cold Is It?

Antarctica is the coldest place on Earth. The lowest temperature ever recorded there was less than

minus 90°C

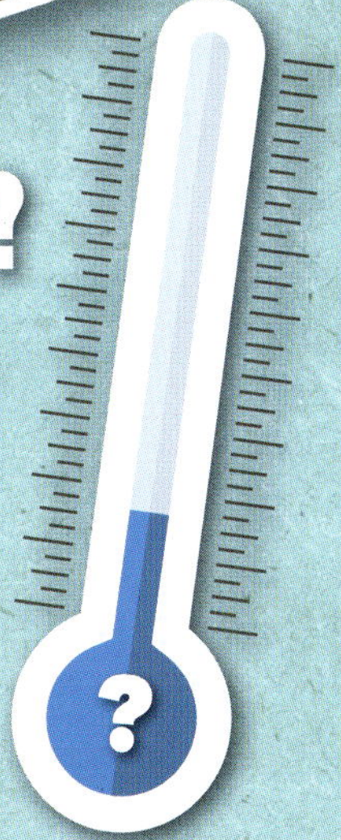

The snow, ice and blizzards make it a lethal place for people who do not have the proper clothing, shelter and survival equipment. Antarctica is also a desert. The temperatures are nearly always below freezing, so the fresh water exists as ice, which living things cannot use for their life processes.

Despite the weather conditions, Antarctica has a thriving wildlife population visiting and living on its continental edges.

Where is Antarctica?

Antarctica is located over the South Pole. It is completely surrounded by oceans.

Latitude

The imaginary horizontal circles drawn around the Earth are called lines of latitude. There are 180 of these circles, and each one is called a degree. The numbering of the lines starts at 0° at the Equator, and moves by one degree until it reaches the South Pole. Here there is no line, just a point which is called 90°. The same numbering of lines of latitude occurs between the Equator and the North Pole.

Longitude

The imaginary lines of longitude are drawn across the globe from the North to the South Poles. There are 360 of these lines and each one is called a degree. At the Equator, the lines are far apart from each other, but at the poles the lines all converge to one point.

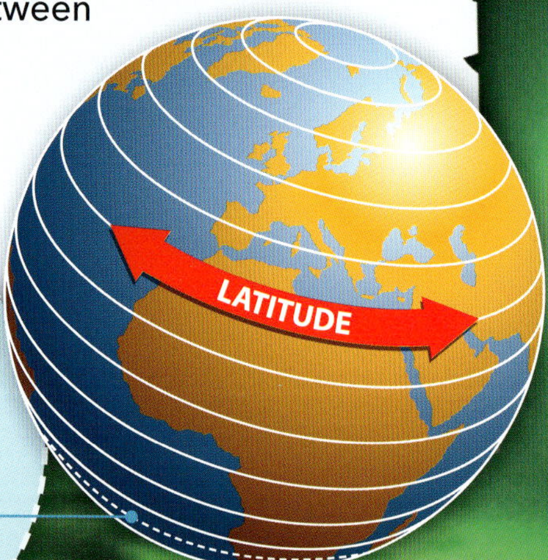

Antarctic Circle

The circle of latitude that is 66.5° south of the Equator marks the boundary of Antarctica. This line is called the Antarctic Circle.

Auroras

The auroras are magnificent, natural light shows that appear in the sky at Earth's North and South Poles. The bands of coloured light in the sky follow the lines of magnetic force coming from the poles.

Roald Amundsen

The Amundsen-Scott South Pole Station

Robert Scott

Amundsen-Scott South Pole Station

In 1911, Roald Amundsen was the first explorer to reach the South Pole, closely followed by Robert Scott who died during his return expedition. In 1956, the Amundsen-Scott South Pole Station was built and named in their honour, near the site of the red and white striped pole that marks the location of the geographic South Pole. The station is the largest and southernmost scientific research facility in Antarctica.

The South Pole

There are two different South Poles

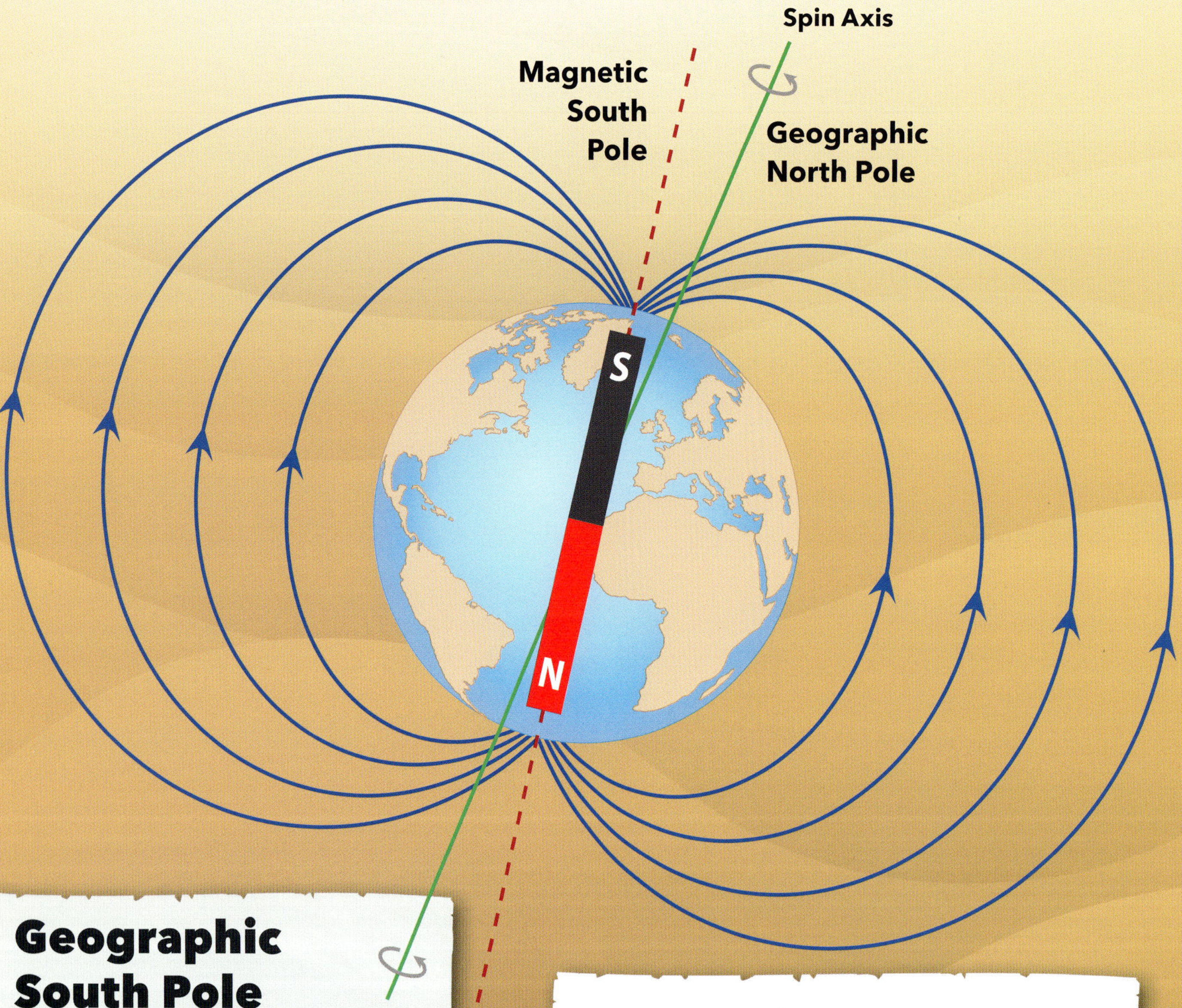

Geographic South Pole

The South Pole we see on a map is at the centre of the smallest ring of latitude which mapmakers draw around the globe. It is also where the Earth's line or axis of rotation meets the surface.

Magnetic North Pole

The magnetic North Pole is a few kilometres away from the geographic South Pole. It marks the place on Earth where lines of magnetic force leave the surface. Earth is a bit like a very big magnet travelling through space, and it is surrounded by lines of magnetic force.

Claiming the Land

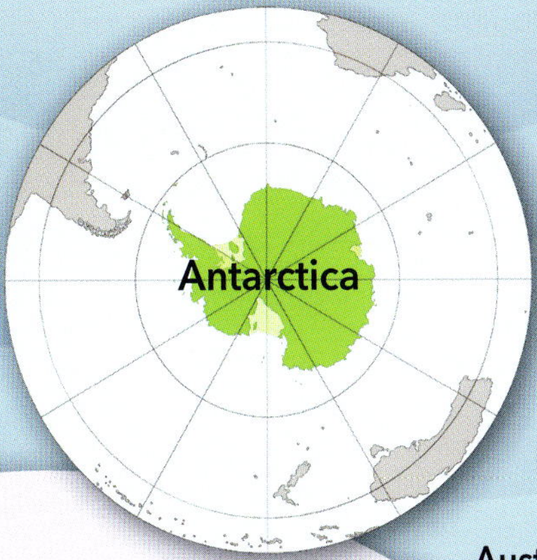

Territorial Claims

It is a rarity to have a piece of land on Earth that is not officially owned by any nation, but this is the situation in Antarctica. There are seven countries that have claimed territory in Antarctica, but none of them currently own any part of it.

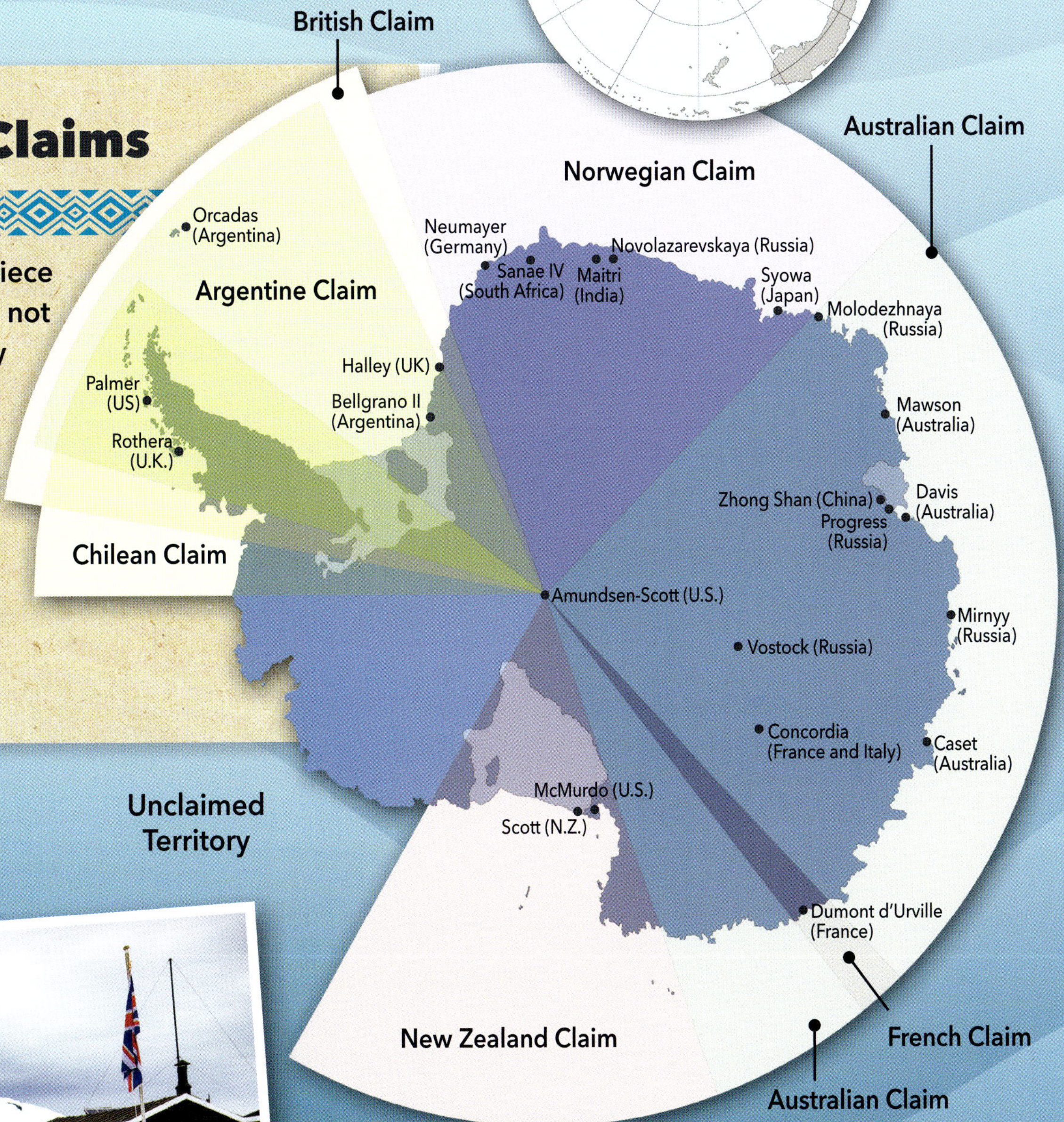

International Bases

Many more countries have built bases in Antarctica without making official territorial claims.

Antarctica's Continental Shelf

The continental shelf around Antarctica is different from shelves in other places on Earth. Over millions of years, the bottoms of glaciers have worn the shelf down to a deeper level than is found around other continents.

Where a continent is bounded by an ocean, the land at the ocean's edge often continues under the water as a continental shelf. This shelf may end abruptly at a point where the underwater rocks drop down to a deep ocean abyss.

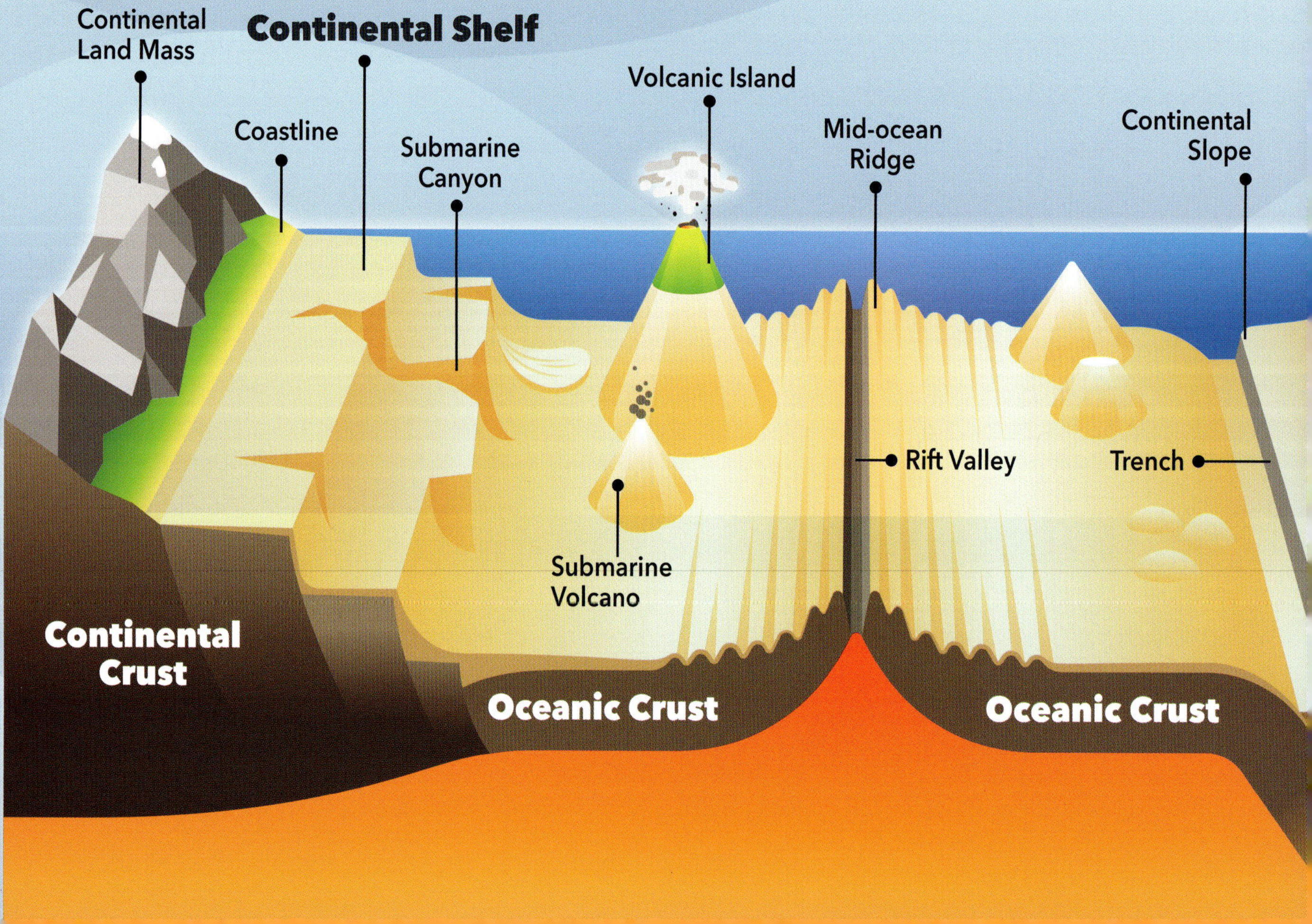

UNCLOS

The United Nations Convention on the Law of the Sea (UNCLOS) sets rules that countries use to determine who has control over the water and the seafloor at a nation's ocean boundary.

Who owns Antarctica's continental shelves?

At an ocean boundary, a nation that is part of a larger continent can claim control over the ocean and the continental shelf for a distance of 200 nautical miles from the shore. This distance is set by member countries of the United Nations under the UNCLOS agreement. No nation officially owns any part of Antarctica, so the application of this rule to the continent of Antarctica is currently not formalised.

Living in Antarctica

No Permanent Population

Antarctica has no permanent human population. Apart from tourists who come for short visits, the only other human inhabitants are scientists and support staff who visit as part of their nation's commitment to undertake research.

Teamwork and Cooperation

Living in such an extreme environment requires extensive planning and organisation just to survive. People need to be able to get along with each other while staying together in small buildings, since they cannot just leave at any time. They also have to stay indoors for long periods if there is a wild, Antarctic storm blowing outside.

A scientific research station in Antarctica

Pollution in Antarctica

There are about 4,000 scientists and researchers who stay in Antarctica during the summer. The control of their rubbish, human waste and chemical pollution is a large part of their daily activities. Antarctica is a pristine wilderness, so anything produced by human activity is a potential polluting threat. This includes exhaust from vehicles or smoke from cigarettes.

Icebreaker ships deliver supplies and remove waste from Antarctica

Some waste is returned to the country of origin, but some is processed in Antarctica. Each country with a research station in Antarctica is expected to control its waste production there to a very high standard.

Wilderness and the Ozone Hole

A Very Special Place

As one of the last great wildernesses on Earth, the Antarctic is a very special place. Even though most of it is inaccessible and inhospitable for people, the unspolied environment is a rarity.

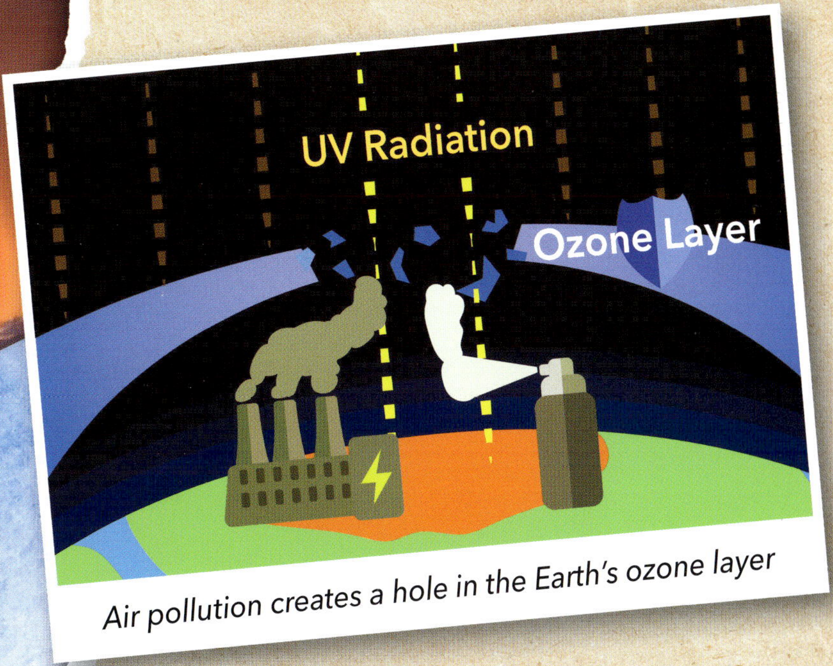

Air pollution creates a hole in the Earth's ozone layer

Ozone Hole

Ozone is a gas in the atmosphere. Its presence helps to protect all living things from too much damaging radiation from the Sun.

Using polluting gases such as we find in some spray cans causes a hole to appear in the ozone layer over the Antarctic. This hole appears around August every year and then reduces a few months later.

Polluting gases found in some spray cans cause damage to the ozone layer

Ice Shelves

As well as having a rocky continental shelf beneath the ice, Antarctica also has ice shelves that extend for many kilometres out on top of the surrounding ocean.

Melting Movements

Ice shelves slow down the flow of glaciers into the ocean. Recent warm temperatures have caused melting of some of the ice shelves around Antarctica, allowing more water from glaciers to enter the ocean.

Ross Ice Shelf is approximately 470,000 square kilometres in area

Antarctica has many large ice shelves. The two largest ones are:

Filchner-Ronne Ice Shelf at about 422,000 square kilometres in area

Icebergs

Around the edges of Antarctica, there are large shelves of ice and also places where glaciers meet the ocean. When pieces of this ice break off they form icebergs in a process called calving. Some icebergs are enormous.

A melting iceberg can release large amounts of nutrients into the ocean, contributing to the growth of microscopic marine life. Icebergs also provide resting places for marine mammals such as seals and penguins.

Hidden Threats

Icebergs are a threat to shipping in the oceans around Antarctica. Most of the iceberg is under the surface of the water and will damage the hull of a ship that comes into contact with it.

Glaciers

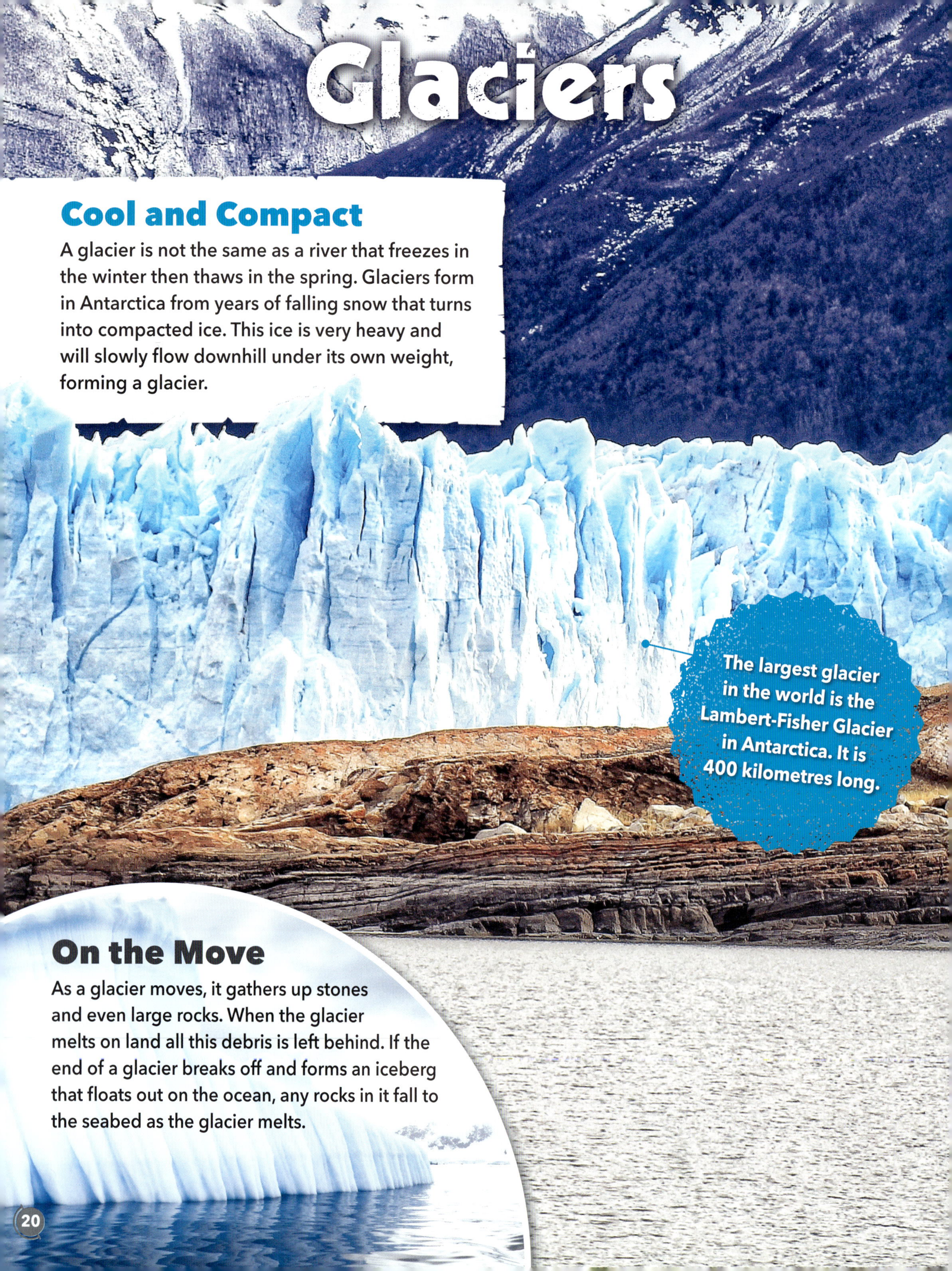

Cool and Compact

A glacier is not the same as a river that freezes in the winter then thaws in the spring. Glaciers form in Antarctica from years of falling snow that turns into compacted ice. This ice is very heavy and will slowly flow downhill under its own weight, forming a glacier.

The largest glacier in the world is the Lambert-Fisher Glacier in Antarctica. It is 400 kilometres long.

On the Move

As a glacier moves, it gathers up stones and even large rocks. When the glacier melts on land all this debris is left behind. If the end of a glacier breaks off and forms an iceberg that floats out on the ocean, any rocks in it fall to the seabed as the glacier melts.

Antarctica and Climate Change

The annual cycles of weather in the Antarctic affect climate conditions in parts of the Earth that are thousands of kilometres away.

Ice Shelves

The ice shelves and surrounding sea ice reflect sunlight, keeping the temperatures in the region lower. As this ice melts, there is less reflection and water can become warmer. Since the warm and cold water in Antarctica affect global circulations in many oceans, this might change temperatures across the water in regions that are far away from Antarctica.

Wildlife

Antarctic wildlife has evolved to survive in a certain temperature range and in an ice and snow-covered environment. The effect of changes in their habitat due to unusual melting of the snow and ice is yet to be documented in detail.

Glaciers

Warmer temperatures allow glaciers to flow more quickly to the oceans. Very large amounts of this melting, glacial water would have an effect on sea levels.

Sunny Nights, Dark Days

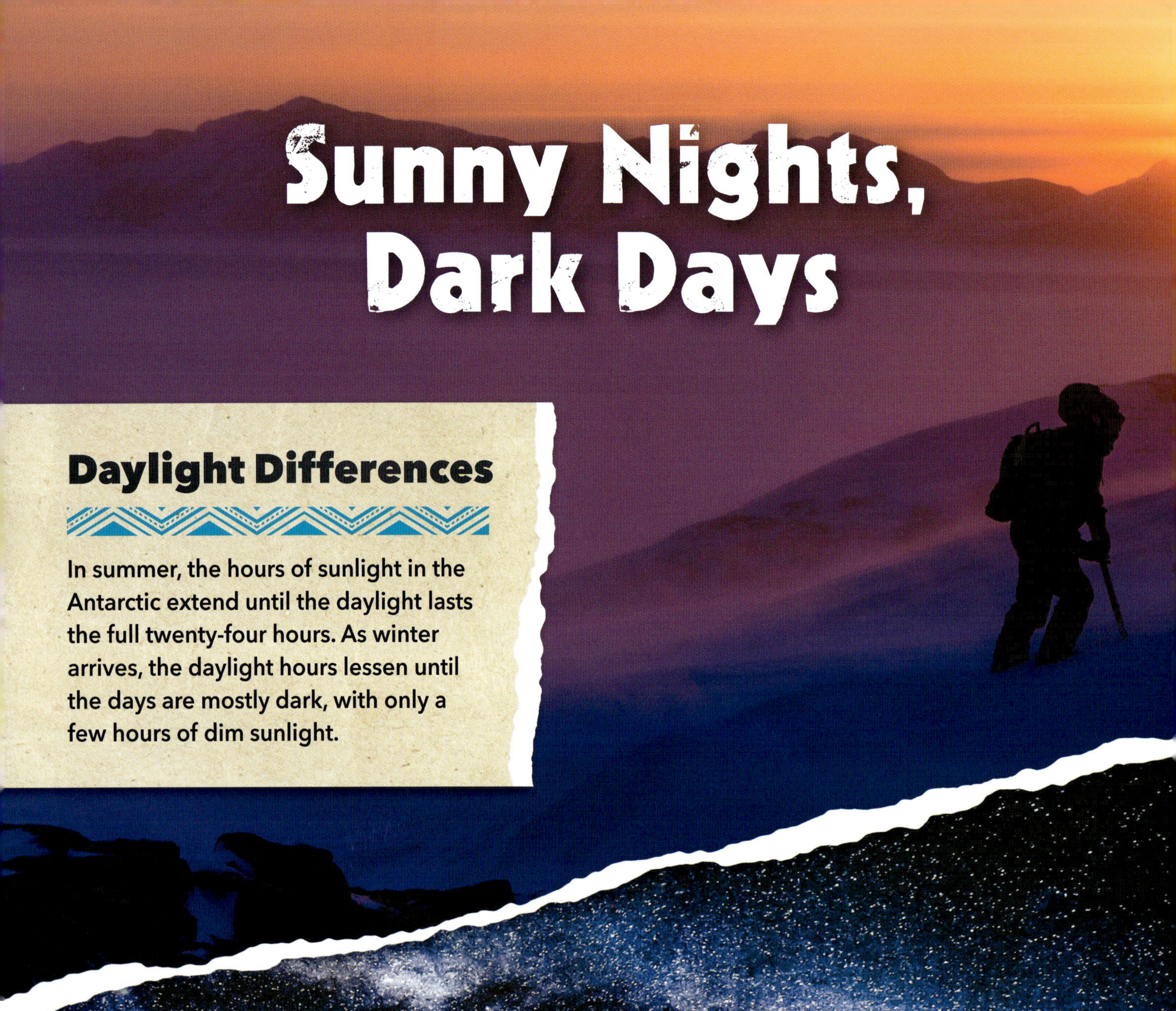

Daylight Differences

In summer, the hours of sunlight in the Antarctic extend until the daylight lasts the full twenty-four hours. As winter arrives, the daylight hours lessen until the days are mostly dark, with only a few hours of dim sunlight.

The *Cygnus Nebula* supernova remnant viewed from Antarctica at night.

Midnight Sun

For a few months of each year, in the middle of summer, the Sun never sets in Antarctica. People refer to the Midnight Sun at this time of year.

Growing food in the Antarctic

Question: With no sunlight, how do scientists living in the Antarctic grow any fresh vegetables to eat during the many months of their stay?

Answer: They grow their plants indoors with artificial lighting using hydroponics.

Antarctic Treaty

Many countries have claimed parts of the Antarctic for their own nations, but none of these claims are formally recognised internationally. The Antarctic Treaty is an agreement between fifty-four nations on the way the Antarctic should be managed.

Mining (such as the facility pictured above in the Arctic circle) is banned in Antarctica

Mining

The land under the Antarctic ice is rich in many resources and minerals. This makes control of the land of interest to nations that would consider mining in the Antarctic if this were ever allowed.

Antarctic Tourism

Tourist Numbers

Over 50,000 tourists visit the Antarctic annually by ship. Some enjoy flights over the area, but do not land. All tourist activities are strictly controlled under the Antarctic Treaty. These controls are to protect the wildlife and to prevent the introduction of diseases and polluting substances. Permits are needed to enter some very sensitive areas.

Warning!
Official tourist advice for Antarctica is "Do not expect a rescue service"

The Internet

Antarctica is an unusual continent in many ways. It even has its own internet country code: **.aq**

Antarctic Wildlife

Vertebrate Animals

These animals all depend on food from the sea, so they are either aquatic or live near the coast. The only mammal to stay in the Antarctic over the long, dark winter is the emperor penguin. Some Antarctic vertebrates are:

- flying birds
- fish
- penguins
- sea lions
- seals
- whales

Penguins at play

Humpback whale

Deschampsia antarctica is one of only two flowering plants native to Antarctica

Plants

Despite the cold climate, there are a few plants that managc to grow on rocky areas. These include:

- fungi
- lichens
- mosses

Seal soaking up sunshine

Wandering albatross

Algae discolours an iceberg

Microscopic Creatures

Antarctic microscopic creatures include:

- algae
- bacteria
- viruses

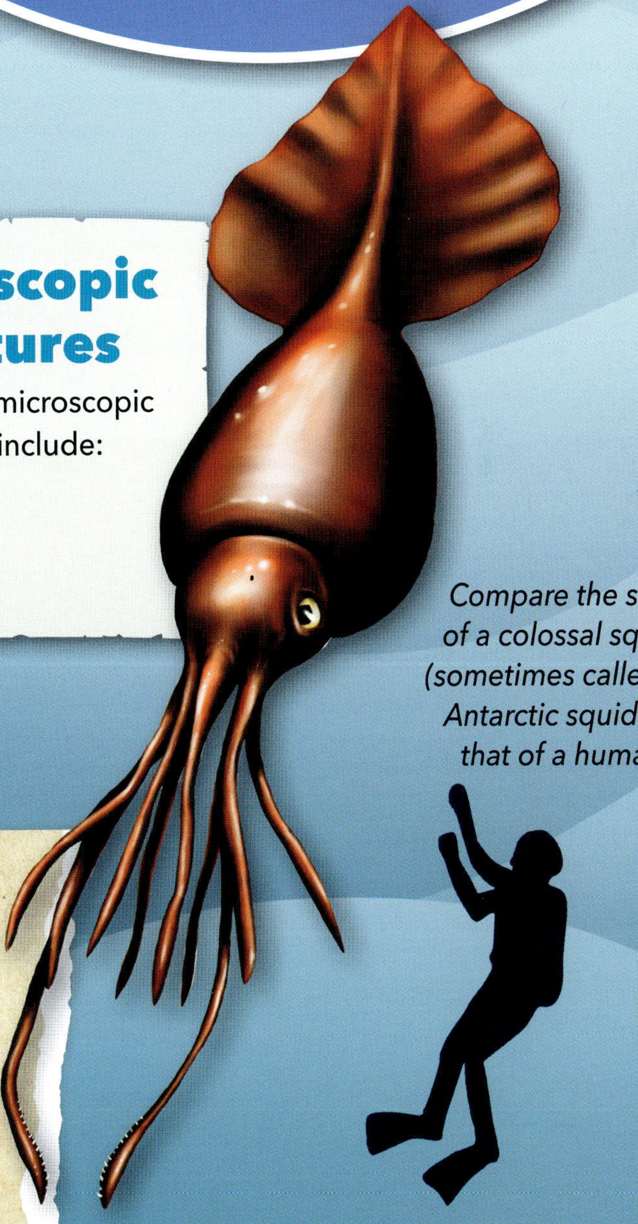

Compare the size of a colossal squid (sometimes called an Antarctic squid) to that of a human

Invertebrates

Some Antarctic invertebrates are:

- flies
- krill
- mites
- sponges
- squids
- worms

Mountains and Volcanoes

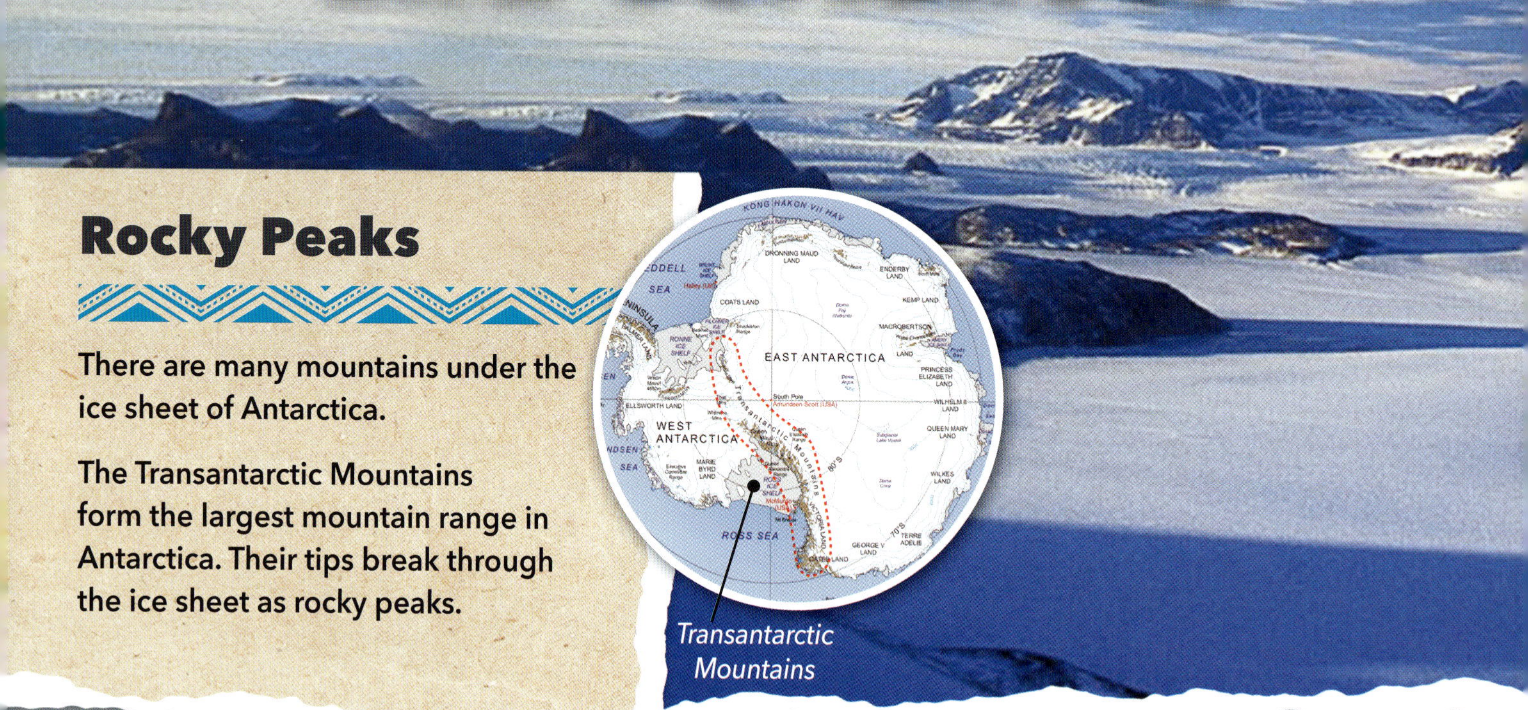

Rocky Peaks

There are many mountains under the ice sheet of Antarctica.

The Transantarctic Mountains form the largest mountain range in Antarctica. Their tips break through the ice sheet as rocky peaks.

Transantarctic Mountains

Mount Sidley

Mount Sidley is the tallest volcano in the Antarctic, at over 4,000 metres high. It is currently dormant.

Below the ice sheets of Antarctica, there are many more dormant volcanoes.

The Dugdale and Murray Glacier (pictured in 1957)

The Thiel Mountains

Mount Erebus

Mount Erebus is a large, active volcano. It is nearly 4,000 metres high and has a pool of hot lava in its crater. Mount Erebus is on Ross Island, which was formed by volcanic activity.

Abandoned whaling station at Grytviken in the Antarctic region

Commercial Fishing

Grytviken whaling station in 1916

Fishy Business

Ever since whalers began hunting whales in the Antarctic region, commercial fishing has attracted ships to the southern oceans. Today, krill and toothfish are the main catches. If you swallow krill as a vitamin supplement, it has probably come from the Antarctic.

Krill

Krill vitamin supplements

Glossary

A glacier is a slow moving mass of compacted ice and snow

compacted packed together tightly

converge come together in one place

debris pieces of rubble or rocks

dormant volcano volcano that is not erupting but may erupt in the future

glacier slowly moving mass of compacted ice and snow

hull bottom of a ship

hydroponics method of growing plants without soil and sometimes with artificial lighting

ice sheet very large, permanent ice cover over land

lethal causing death

nautical mile term used to measure distance over water or when travelling in the air. It measures 1.85 kilometres

ocean abyss very deep part of an ocean

plate tectonics movement of large blocks of land across the Earth

pristine very clean and unspoiled

thaw melt

Hydroponics is a method of growing plants without soil that sometimes uses artificial lighting

Ice shelves

Index

Aurora